Sanjeev Kapoor's

Pickles, Chutneys 'n' More

In association with Alyona Kapoor

Popular Prakashan
www.popularprakashan.com

Published by
POPULAR PRAKASHAN PVT. LTD.
301, Mahalaxmi Chambers
22, Bhulabhai Desai Road
Mumbai - 400 026
for KHANA KHAZANA PUBLICATIONS PVT. LTD.

First Published 2009

(4303)
ISBN: 978-81-7991-555-4

Design: Anjali Sawant
Photography: Bharat Bhirangi

PRINTED IN INDIA
by Azure Press Service
A-28, Naraina Ind. Area
Phase 1, New Delhi - 28.

AUTHOR'S NOTE

Pickles, chutneys, sauces and dips are usually not eaten on their own but they form an important part of the menu. They enhance the flavour of other foods and make them more appetising.

Indian cooking is adept at turning different fruits and vegetables - ranging from mangoes and limes to tomatoes, carrots and radishes - into an amazing variety of pickles and chutneys. Even greens like spinach find their way into tasty chutneys!

'Pickling' means 'preserving'. The vegetable or fruit is immersed in brine, or in a mixture of condiments and oil, so that it remains unspoilt for a long duration. The ideal pickling season is summer when home-made pickles are prepared and kept in the sun for at least three weeks before use.

The masala consists of acidic ingredients besides spices and these retard the bacterial grown while the oil and salt act as preservatives. Pickles will remain fresh and unspoilt as long as they do not come into contact with moisture. Preservatives like citric acid and sodium benzoate are used in the commercially produced pickles.

Sterilized porcelain or glass jars with airtight lids are used for storage. To sterilize the jars or bottles, rinse with boiling water and dry in the sun. Alternatively, you can heat in a water bath on medium heat for fifteen minutes, dry and use them.

Chutney originated in India and was introduced to the western world by the British when they took it back with them to England, along with some of the other popular Indian dishes like curries.

In India, chutney is often made for instant consumption without the use of any preservative. But when it is to be stored, then a preservative like vinegar or citric acid is added. Chutney can be dry or wet, thick and chunky or smooth. Dry chutney comes in the form of coarse or smooth powder. Then again it can be either cooked or uncooked. Chillies form an integral part of most chutney recipes. The taste could range from very sweet to very spicy.

A sauce is either a liquid or semi-solid which is used in the preparation of other foods. Normally a sauce is not consumed by itself but used to add flavour, moisture and visual appeal to a dish. 'Sauce' is a French word derived from the Latin salsus, which means 'salted'. In French cuisine sauces have been used since the Middle Ages and one can find hundreds of sauces in their culinary repertoire.

Sauces can be freshly-prepared, like Béchamel Sauce or like Soy or Worcestershire sauce, can be bought ready-made. Salad dressings are sauces that are used to enhance salads. In practice sauces are classified into four families each of which has a mother sauce from which other derivatives are made. They are Béchamel, based on milk thickened with a white roux (Roux is the thickening agent used in four of the mother sauces. It is a cooked mixture of equal parts of wheat flour and fat, traditionally clarified butter.); Espagnole, based on brown stock (usually veal or the meat of young calf), thickened with a brown roux; Velouté, based on a white stock, thickened with a blonde roux and Allemande, based on velouté sauce, thickened with egg yolks and heavy cream.

A dip or dipping sauce literally means a type of condiment in which other foods are dipped and consumed. Dips are commonly used for finger foods such as pita bread, dumplings, raw vegetables fingers (crudités), fried pieces of seafood or meat, potato or tortilla chips and other foods that can be easily held. In this book, you will find a wide range of recipes that will appeal to a wide variety of tastes.

There are spicy and sweet chutneys like Dal Thuvayal, Tomato Chutney, Fig and Date Chutney, Sweet Mango Chutney and Plum Chutney; tongue-tickling pickles such as Gunda Kairi, Methamba, Kairi ki Launjee and Goan Chilli Pickle; sauces like Hot Garlic Sauce, Sichuan Sauce and Black Bean Sauce; and last but not least, dips such as Melting Cheese Dip, Thousand Island Dip and Salsa Fresca!

Happy Cooking!

CONTENTS

Teekha Nimbu Achaar

Ingredients

6 large lemons, quartered and seeded
¼ cup salt
½ cup sugar
2 inches ginger, crushed
8 green chillies, chopped
2-3 tablespoons red chilli powder
1 tablespoon roasted mustard seeds
1 teaspoon roasted fenugreek seeds
2 star anise, roasted

Method

1. Place the lemons in a large bowl and sprinkle salt over it. Cover and leave it for one day. On the following day, toss the lemons in the juice.
2. Take four quarters of the salted lemons and squeeze out the juice in a small pan. Add the sugar, ginger and three tablespoons water. Bring to a boil, and cook on low heat, stirring continuously, till the sugar dissolves completely. Add the green chillies and chilli powder. Cook for one minute. Set aside and allow it to cool.
3. Add the roasted mustard seeds, roasted fenugreek seeds and roasted star anise. Mix well. Pour the remaining lemon quarters into a sterilized glass jar. Pour over the sugar-chillies mix, covering them completely. Press the lemons down so that they are soaked completely. Cover the jar with a lid and set aside for twenty-five to twenty-eight days for the pickle to mature.

Baingan Ka Achaar

Ingredients

1 large brinjal, cut into ½-inch cubes
3 tablespoons sea salt
1 tablespoon mustard seeds
2 two-inch pieces fresh ginger, peeled and chopped
12 garlic cloves, peeled and chopped
2 cups vinegar
2 cups mustard oil
1 tablespoon turmeric powder
2 tablespoons salt
1 cup sugar
25 green chillies, cut into ½-inch pieces

Method

1. Mix the brinjals with the sea salt and set aside for four hours.
2. Grind the mustard seeds with ginger, garlic and two tablespoons of vinegar.
3. Heat the mustard oil in a pan on medium heat and stir-fry the ground spices.
4. Add the turmeric powder, remaining vinegar, salt, sugar and green chillies. Squeeze the brinjal cubes to remove excess liquid, and add to the above mixture.
5. Cook till dry and the oil rises to the surface. Cool and store in a sterilized bottle.

Mixed Vegetable Pickle

Ingredients

500 grams carrots, cut into 1½-inch pieces

500 grams cauliflower, separated into medium-sized florets

500 grams turnips, cut into 1½-inch pieces

12 tablespoons mustard oil

6 tablespoons coarsely ground ginger paste

6 tablespoons coarsely ground garlic paste

1½ tablespoons mustard seeds, powdered

1½ tablespoons red chilli powder

½ tablespoon *garam masala* powder

½ tablespoon black peppercorns, coarsely powdered

¾ cup jaggery, grated

1 tablespoon salt

1½ tablespoons vinegar

Method

1. Heat the oil in a *kadai*. Add the ginger and garlic and cook till light golden.
2. Add the mustard, chilli, *garam masala* and peppercorn powders, and sauté for a few seconds.
3. Add the jaggery and salt and mix. Add the vegetables, mix and cook for three to four minutes.
4. Remove from the heat and set aside to cool completely. Add the vinegar and mix. Store in a sterilized bottle.

Mirchicha Thecha

Ingredients

8-9 green chillies, roughly chopped

1 tablespoon oil

¼ cup white sesame seeds

7-8 garlic cloves, roughly chopped

½ cup grated coconut,

1 tablespoon fresh coriander, roughly chopped

Salt to taste

Method

1. Heat the oil on a *tawa*, add the green chillies, sesame seeds, garlic, coconut and fresh coriander. Sauté for three to four minutes.
2. Remove from heat and set aside to cool. Add the salt and mix.
3. Grind coarsely in a blender or pound in a mortar with a pestle.
4. Serve as an accompaniment

Andhra Avakkai

Ingredients

12 medium unripe green mangoes

1 cup mustard seeds

2 cups red chilli powder

1½ cups salt

¼ cup turmeric powder

¼ teaspoon asafoetida

4 tablespoons fenugreek seeds

2 cups sesame oil

Method

1. Select good, firm and sour mangoes. Wash thoroughly and wipe them completely dry with an absorbent kitchen towel. Cut the mangoes into half with the seed and then further cut each half into six to eight equal-sized pieces.
2. Spread them on a mat and dry in the sun for about two days. Clean and dry the mustard seeds and pound to a coarse powder.
3. Mix thoroughly the chilli powder, salt, turmeric powder, asafoetida, mustard powder, fenugreek seeds and oil. Discard the seeds from the sun-dried mango and add to the pickle mixture.

4. Transfer the pickle to a ceramic pickle jar, cover the mouth with a piece of muslin, fastened with a string and keep in the sun for three days without stirring.
5. From the fourth day onwards, stir the pickle well and continue to keep in the sun for at least a week to ten days.
6. This pickle will last for a year if kept well.

Chef's Tip

Use only good quality white sesame oil for the pickle.
Freshly pounded or milled chilli powder is recommended.
You may also add ¼ cup chickpeas along with the mangoes.

Keri Ki Launjee

Ingredients

1 kilogram unripe green mangoes
3 tablespoons mustard oil
¾ teaspoon fenugreek seeds
4 teaspoons fennel seeds
½ teaspoon onion seeds
1 teaspoon coriander powder
1 teaspoon red chilli powder
½ teaspoon turmeric powder
Salt to taste
1¼ cups grated jaggery

Method

1. Peel the mangoes, cut lengthways into quarters and remove the kernels.
2. Heat the oil in a *kadai* to smoking point. Lower the heat to medium, add the fenugreek seeds and sauté till they begin to change colour.
3. Add the fennel seeds, onion seeds, coriander powder, chilli powder, turmeric powder and salt. Mix well.
4. Add the mangoes and sauté for five minutes. Add the jaggery and half a cup of water. Bring to a boil, cover the pan and simmer, stirring occasionally, for seven or eight minutes.
5. Remove and cool. Store in a sterilized bottle.

Goan Chilli Pickle

Ingredients

500 grams mild green chillies

½ cup salt

8-10 dried red Reshampatti chillies

1 cup vinegar

200 grams garlic, peeled and chopped

200 grams fresh ginger, peeled and chopped

½ cup Tamarind Pulp (page 42)

1 cup sesame oil

¾ cup sugar

1 teaspoon split fenugreek seeds, powdered

Method

1. Crush the green chillies with a little salt in a blender. Soak the red chillies in vinegar.
2. Crush the garlic and ginger. Grind the red chillies with the vinegar and tamarind pulp.
3. Heat the oil in a pan to smoking point. Cool slightly and add the crushed garlic, ginger and green chillies and sauté on high heat for four to five minutes.
4. Add the red chilli paste and continue to cook, stirring continuously, for another four to five minutes. Add the sugar and salt and stir. Add the powdered fenugreek seeds and mix well. Cook a little longer. Transfer to a sterilized bottle and leave to cool. Store in a refrigerator.

Methamba (Mango and Fenugreek Seed Pickle)

Ingredients

3-4 medium unripe green mangoes
1 teaspoon fenugreek seeds
Salt to taste
6-8 cloves
2 one-inch cinnamon sticks
1 cup oil
1 teaspoon mustard seeds
¼ teaspoon asafoetida
5-6 dried red chillies, stems removed
2¼ cups jaggery, grated

Method

1. Wash the mangoes and wipe them dry. Peel and cut into halves. Remove the seeds and cut into one-inch pieces. Rub the salt and set aside for twenty-four hours. Wash the mangoes and wipe them completely dry.
2. Grind the cloves and cinnamon to a coarse powder. Heat the oil in a pan, add the mustard seeds and when they splutter, add the asafoetida, fenugreek seeds and dried chillies. Stir-fry briefly. Add the mangoes and jaggery.
3. Cook on medium heat for five to six minutes or till the jaggery melts completely and coats the mangoes.
4. Remove from heat and sprinkle coarsely ground cloves and cinnamon. Mix thoroughly and store the *methamba* in a sterilized airtight bottle.

Elamcha Urga (Lemon Pickle)

Ingredients

10 lemons

2 tablespoons vinegar

1½ tablespoons salt

3½ tablespoons sugar

4 garlic cloves

1 inch ginger

225 grams dates, seeded and roughly chopped

4 tablespoons oil

1 teaspoon cumin seeds

2 teaspoons mustard seeds

2 tablespoons red chilli powder

Method

1. Wash, wipe dry and quarter the lemons and remove all the pips. Place them in a pan along with the vinegar, salt and sugar. Cover the pan and simmer over low heat until the lemons have softened. Remove the lemons and reserve the liquid. Wipe the garlic and ginger dry and grind along with the dates.
2. Heat the oil in a pan and sauté the cumin seeds and mustard seeds. Remove from heat and add the reserved liquid. Add the chilli powder and return to heat and stir for a minute.
3. Slowly add the ground dates-ginger-garlic and one-fourth cup of water and mix. Add the lemons and boil for a few minutes. Allow to cool and pour into a sterilized jar. Seal while warm.

Lemon Pickle

Ingredients

15 -18 medium lemons

4 one-inch ginger pieces, finely chopped

10-12 green chillies, cut into ½-inch pieces

1 teaspoon fenugreek seeds

½ teaspoon asafoetida powder

6 tablespoons sesame oil

1 teaspoon mustard seeds

¼ teaspoon turmeric powder

Salt to taste

Method

1. Wash and soak the lemons in hot water for half an hour. Drain, wipe them dry and cut them into two. Remove the seeds and cut each half into four to five pieces. Dry-roast the fenugreek seeds. Cool, grind to a coarse powder and mix with the asafoetida powder.
2. Heat the oil in a pan, add the mustard seeds and stir-fry till it crackles. Add the ginger and green chillies and sauté for two minutes. Add the lemons, turmeric powder and salt. Reduce the heat and cook for ten minutes, stirring frequently.
3. Sprinkle the fenugreek and asafoetida powder. Stir well and remove from heat.
4. Cool, pour into a sterilized bottle and store in a refrigerator.

Amla Pickle

Ingredients

500 grams Indian gooseberries

1½ cups sea salt

1 teaspoon turmeric powder

275 ml sesame oil

1 teaspoon asafoetida

1½ cups red chilli powder

3 tablespoons mustard powder

Method

1. Cut each gooseberry into thin segments. Add one cup of salt and half a teaspoon of turmeric powder. Stir and store, covered, in a glass bottle for two to three days. Shake the bottle daily a couple of times, but do not use a spoon or stir by hand.
2. Heat the oil to smoking point and leave to cool slightly. Add the asafoetida and mix well. Set aside to cool the oil a little more. Crush the remaining sea salt in a bowl.
3. Add the chilli powder, remaining turmeric powder and mustard powder and mix well. Add the gooseberries along with the juice collected in the bottle. Mix well.
4. Add the cooled oil to the gooseberry mixture. Transfer the pickle to a sterilized glass or porcelain bottle and seal tightly. The pickle will be ready for consumption in three to four days and will keep for at least three to four months.

Aam Ka Achaar

Ingredients

500 grams unripe green mangoes
2½ tablespoons fennel seeds
1 tablespoon fenugreek seeds
2 teaspoons onion seeds
2½ teaspoons turmeric powder
2 tablespoons red chilli powder
2 teaspoons skinless split mustard seeds
3½ teaspoons salt
¼ cup chickpeas
1 cup mustard oil

Method

1. Wash and wipe the mangoes dry. Peel and cut them into half, remove the seeds and then cut into half-inch cubes. Grind the fennel seeds and fenugreek seeds to a powder.
2. Place the mangoes in a bowl, add the fennel seed and fenugreek seed powders, onion seeds, turmeric powder, chilli powder, split mustard seeds, salt and chickpeas. Mix well.
3. Heat the mustard oil in a pan to smoking point, remove and let it cool completely. Add the cooled oil to the mangoes and mix well so that the pieces are coated with the oil. Leave the pickle to stand, covered, for three days. On the fourth day transfer the pickle to a sterlized porcelain jar.
4. Cover the mouth of the jar with a piece of muslin, fastened with a string. Place the jar in the sun for twelve to fifteen days to mature. Remember to shake the contents at least once a day.
5. The pickle will be ready for consumption on the twelfth day and will last for one year if stored in a cool, dry place.

Gunda Kairi

Ingredients

2 kilograms *gunda*
1½ kilograms unripe, green mangoes
1½ cups sea salt, ground
2 teaspoons turmeric powder
3 cups split mustard seeds
1 cup split fenugreek seeds
2 cups Kashmiri chilli powder
1 cup Reshampatti chilli powder
1 tablespoon asafoetida
20-24 black peppercorns
½ kilogram groundnut oil

Method

1. Apply a little oil and salt to your hands before handling the *gunda*. Split the *gunda* and remove the seeds.
2. Wash, wipe dry and cut the mangoes into medium cubes.
3. Place the mangoes and *gunda* in a large bowl. Add one cup of sea salt and one teaspoon of turmeric powder and mix well. Cover and set aside for half an hour.
4. Mix together the mustard seeds, fenugreek seeds, Kashmiri and Reshampatti chilli powders, asafoetida, peppercorns, remaining sea salt and turmeric powder.

5. Heat half the groundnut oil to smoking point. Cool slightly and add to the mixed spices.
6. Discard the water released by the mangoes and *gunda* mixture. Add the mango and *gunda* mixture to the spices and mix well. Transfer to sterilized glass or porcelain jar, packing the pickle in tightly to remove any air bubbles. Cover and set aside for twenty-four hours.
7. Heat the remaining oil to smoking point, cool and add to the pickle. Cover and leave to mature for at least ten to fifteen days. Three weeks is ideal, by which time the oil will rise to the surface and the pickle will be ready for consumption.

Note: Gunda is a Rajasthani berry.

Gor Keri

Ingredients

1 kilogram unripe green mangoes, peeled and cut into ½-inch cubes

6 teaspoons salt

1 teaspoon turmeric powder

1 kilogram grated jaggery

200 grams pickle *masala*

1 tablespoon fennel seeds

Pickle masala

100 grams split mustard seeds, lightly roasted

100 grams split fenugreek seeds, lightly roasted

100 grams split coriander seeds, lightly roasted

300 grams red chilli powder

½ teaspoon turmeric powder

1 teaspoon asafoetida

¼ cup oil, heated to smoking point and cooled

Method

1. For the pickle *masala*, combine the mustard, fenugreek and coriander seeds, chilli powder, turmeric powder and asafoetida in a deep bowl and mix. Add the oil and mix again. You can store this in an airtight jar to be used when required.

2. Add the salt and one teaspoon turmeric powder to the mango cubes in a large glass bowl and mix well. Cover and set aside for five to six hours. During this time, the mango cubes will release water.
3. Drain the mango cubes, spread them on a large plate and dry in the sun for about six hours.
4. Place the dried mango cubes in a large glass bowl. Add the jaggery, pickle *masala* and fennel seeds and mix well. Cover and set aside for six to eight days stirring twice daily till all the jaggery has melted. Store in a sterilized airtight glass or porcelain jar.

Chef's Tip

Gor keri, in literal translation, means jaggery mango...that is true of this typical Gujarati pickle as unripe green mangoes are soaked in loads of jaggery! Unripe mangoes are great for reducing acidity and body heat and improving digestion.

Varhadi Thecha

Ingredients

20-25 dried red chillies
2 tablespoons oil
12-16 garlic cloves, roughly chopped
1 inch ginger, roughly chopped
1 tablespoon lemon juice
4 tablespoons vinegar
Salt to taste
½ teaspoon sugar

Method

1. Heat the oil in a pan and add the garlic and ginger.
2. Stir-fry briefly, add the red chillies and continue stir-frying for half a minute more.
3. Remove from heat and cool. Grind with the lemon juice, vinegar, salt and sugar into a fine paste.
4. Serve as an accompaniment.

Chhunda

Ingredients

2 kilograms unripe green mangoes, peeled and grated

4 tablespoons salt

½ teaspoon turmeric powder

2 kilograms sugar

2-3 tablespoons red chilli powder

2 teaspoons cumin powder

Method

1. Add the salt and turmeric powder to the grated mangoes. Mix well and keep aside in a stainless steel or glass vessel for half an hour. Add the sugar and mix well.
2. Transfer the grated mango and sugar mixture to a thick-bottomed vessel. Place the vessel on low heat and cook, stirring constantly. Cook for about thirty to forty minutes or until the water evaporates and a one-string sugar syrup is formed. Remove from heat and let it cool.
3. When cooled, add the chilli and cumin powders and mix well. Store in a dry and sterilized glass jar with a tight lid.

Chef's Tip

Chhunda can be cooked in the sunlight. Place the grated mangoes in a sterilized glass jar and add the salt and turmeric powder. Mix well and add the sugar. Cover the mouth of the jar with a thin piece of muslin, fastened with a string and leave it in the sun till the sugar gets a one-string syrup consistency. Add the chilli and cumin powders and keep again in the sun for a day or two. Remember to stir it daily and bring it back into the house at sunset.

Nimbu Ka Achaar

Ingredients

1 kilogram lemons
5 tablespoons salt
5 tablespoons black salt
3 tablespoons red chilli powder
3 tablespoons *garam masala* powder
5 tablespoons carom seeds
2 cups sugar

Method

1. Wash and wipe the lemons completely dry. Make deep slits crosswise in each lemon without cutting through completely.
2. Place the lemons in a bowl; add the salt, black salt, chilli powder, garam masala powder and carom seeds. Mix well, to coat the lemons evenly with the *masala*. Add the sugar, which should be approximately half the weight of the lemons; mix well.
3. Transfer the lemons into a porcelain container and cover with a piece of muslin, secured with a string. Place the container in the sun for twenty-five to thirty days to allow the pickle to mature.

Note: The *garam masala* should not contain any coriander seeds.

Mint Chutney

Ingredients

3 cups fresh mint, roughly chopped

2 cups fresh coriander, roughly chopped

6 green chillies, chopped

1 medium onion, peeled and roughly chopped

3 inches fresh ginger, peeled and roughly chopped

2 tablespoon lemon juice

Salt to taste

2 tablespoons dried pomegranate seed powder

Method

1. Grind the mint, coriander, green chillies, onion, and ginger to a fine paste, adding a little water if required.
2. Add the lemon juice, salt and dried pomegranate seed powder.
3. Mix well and serve.

Dal Thuvayal

Ingredients

1 cup split Bengal gram, soaked
8 tablespoons oil
½ teaspoon mustard seeds
6 dried red chillies
2 tablespoons coriander seeds
1 teaspoon cumin seeds
15-20 black peppercorns
1 medium onion, sliced
6 garlic cloves, sliced
½ lemon-sized ball tamarind
¼ teaspoon asafoetida
Salt to taste

Method

1. Heat the oil in a pan and add the mustard seeds. When they splutter add the red chillies, coriander seeds, cumin seeds and black peppercorns and sauté for two minutes. Add the onion and garlic and continue sautéing on medium heat for two to three minutes.
2. Add the drained Bengal gram and tamarind and sauté on high heat for two to three minutes. Mix in the asafoetida and salt.
3. Remove from heat and set aside to cool. Grind to a coarse paste, adding a little water, as required. Serve at room temperature.

Sweet Chilli Chutney

Ingredients

18-20 Kashmiri red chillies, broken into bits
3 medium tomatoes, chopped
Salt to taste
8-10 garlic cloves, peeled and chopped
2 tablespoons oil
2 tablespoons sugar
2 tablespoons honey

Method

1. Process the red chillies, tomatoes, half a cup of water, salt and garlic in a blender, to a smooth paste.
2. Heat the oil in a pan, add the paste and cook for a few minutes. Add the sugar and bring to a boil. Cook for ten minutes. Remove the scum if any.
3. Stir in the honey and remove the pan from the heat.
4. Cool and store.

Maharashtrian Coconut Chutney

Ingredients

½ fresh coconut

½ cup fresh coriander, roughly chopped

3-4 garlic cloves, roughly chopped

3 green chillies, roughly chopped

½ tablespoon lemon juice

2 teaspoons sugar

Salt to taste

3 teaspoons yogurt

Method

1. Scrape, grate or cut the fresh coconut into small pieces.
2. Mix all the ingredients except the yogurt and grind to a coarse paste.
3. Mix in the yogurt with the chutney, adjust the seasoning and serve with snacks.

Green Mango And Onion Chutney

Ingredients

3 medium unripe, green mangoes, peeled, stoned and chopped

2 medium onions, grated

4-6 green chillies, chopped

1 tablespoon dried pomegranate seeds

2 tablespoons lemon juice

½ teaspoon black salt

Salt to taste

½ teaspoon sugar

Method

1. Process the unripe, green mangoes, green chillies, dried pomegranate seeds, lemon juice, black salt, salt and sugar in a blender and grind to a smooth paste.
2. Adjust the consistency if required by adding water.
3. Squeeze the grated onion to remove excess juice. Add to the chutney and mix.
4. Serve at room temperature.

Khajur Ki Chutney

Ingredients

15-20 dates

2 teaspoons cumin seeds

¼ teaspoon fennel seeds

½ cup jaggery, grated

1 cup Tamarind Pulp (see below)

2 teaspoons red chilli powder

1 teaspoon dried ginger powder

1 teaspoon black salt

Salt to taste

Method

1. Wash and stone the dates and chop roughly. Dry-roast the cumin seeds and fennel seeds. Cool slightly and grind to a powder. Mix together the dates, jaggery, tamarind pulp, cumin and fennel powder, chilli powder, dried ginger powder, black salt, salt to taste and one cup of water.
2. Cook on medium heat and bring to a boil. Reduce heat and continue to cook for six to eight minutes. Cool and serve.

Tamarind Pulp

Soak 75 grams tamarind in one cup of warm water for 10-15 minutes. Grind to a smooth paste and strain to remove any fibres. Store the pulp in an airtight container in the refrigerator.

Fig And Date Chutney

Ingredients

5 figs, chopped
2 cups dates, chopped
1 medium orange
2 medium onions, peeled and chopped
2 inches fresh ginger, peeled and grated
1 teaspoon red chilli flakes
1½ cups brown sugar
1¼ cups vinegar
Salt to taste

Method

1. Peel the orange and separate the segments. Remove the white part of the peel and cut peel into fine strips.
2. Place the orange segments in a heavy-bottomed pan with the figs and dates. Add the orange peel, onions, ginger, chilli flakes, brown sugar, vinegar and salt.
3. Bring the mixture to a boil, lower heat and simmer for approximately one hour, or until the mixture is thick and pulpy.
4. Transfer the chutney into a warm, sterilized bottle. Seal while still hot.

Sweet Mango Chutney

Ingredients

900 grams slightly ripe mangoes, peeled and thinly sliced

900 grams sugar

4-5 garlic cloves, chopped

1½ inch ginger, chopped

1 teaspoon red chilli powder

1 teaspoon *garam masala* powder

2 tablespoons vinegar

Salt to taste

Method

1. Cook the mango slices with very little water in a pan till soft. Add the sugar and mix well.
2. Tie the garlic, ginger, chilli powder and *garam masala* powder in a piece of muslin to make a loose *potli*; add to the mango mixture. Mix well and cook on medium heat, till the syrup attains one-string consistency.
3. Stir in the vinegar and salt; cook for five minutes.
4. Remove the *potli*, cool and store the chutney in a sterilized glass bottle.

Tamarind Chutney

Ingredients

1 cup seedless tamarind
2 tablespoons raisins
1¼ cups jaggery, grated
1 inch cinnamon
½ teaspoon black salt
1 teaspoon red chilli powder
1 teaspooon roasted cumin powder
1½ teaspoons dried ginger powder
Salt to taste

Method

1. Soak the tamarind in two cups of water. Cook on medium heat for two to three minutes. Let it stand for half an hour. Extract the pulp by straining through a sieve.
2. Wash the raisins and pat them dry. Mix together the jaggery, cinnamon and tamarind pulp in a pan. Cook for half an hour on medium heat.
3. Add the black salt, chilli powder, roasted cumin powder, dried ginger powder and salt to taste. Cook for ten minutes.
4. Add the raisins and cook for five more minutes. Let it cool completely and store in an airtight container.

Fresh Tomato And Onion Chutney

Ingredients

4 medium tomatoes, chopped

1 medium onion, peeled and chopped

1 green chilli, chopped

4 tablespoons fresh coriander, chopped

1 tablespoon lemon juice

½ teaspoon salt

1 teaspoon red chilli powder

½ teaspoon roasted cumin powder

Method

1. Grind together the tomatoes, onion, green chilli, fresh coriander, lemon juice, salt, chilli powder and roasted cumin powder to a coarse paste.
2. Serve immediately.

Chef's Tip

This chutney must be eaten fresh.

Tamatar Ki Chutney - I

Ingredients

7-8 medium ripe tomatoes, finely chopped
2 tablespoons pure ghee
½ teaspoon cumin seeds
A pinch of asafoetida
1 green chilli, chopped
10 curry leaves
½ teaspoon red chilli powder
¼ teaspoon turmeric powder
1 teaspoon coriander powder
½ teaspoon cumin powder
½ teaspoon *garam masala* powder
Salt to taste
1 teaspoon sugar
2 tablespoons chopped fresh coriander

Method

1. Heat the ghee in a pan. Add the cumin seeds and when they begin to change colour, add the asafoetida, green chilli and curry leaves and sauté for a minute.
2. Mix the chilli, turmeric, coriander, cumin and *garam masala* powders in one-fourth cup of water and add to the pan. Sauté for two minutes.
3. Add the tomatoes, salt, sugar and half a cup of water and mix well. Lower the heat once the mixture comes to a boil, and simmer for ten to fifteen minutes. Garnish with fresh coriander and serve hot.

Tamatar Ki Chutney - 2

Ingredients

3 large ripe tomatoes

4 large Bhavnagari chillies

2 tablespoons oil

1 medium onion, chopped

½ teaspoon red chilli powder

5-6 black peppercorns, crushed

Salt to taste

½ teaspoon cumin powder

½ teaspoon *garam masala* powder

2 tablespoons fresh coriander, finely chopped

1 teaspoon sugar

Method

1. Roast the tomatoes and Bhavnagari chillies directly on an open flame. Place them in cold water and peel. Chop the tomatoes and chillies. Heat the oil in a pan. Add the onion and sauté till soft. Add the tomatoes and cook on high heat.
2. Add the chillies, chilli powder, crushed peppercorns, salt, cumin powder and *garam masala* powder. Sauté for a few seconds. Stir in the fresh coriander and sugar. Cook for four to five minutes. Transfer the mixture to a bowl and blend coarsely with a hand-blender.
3. Serve immediately, or cool and store in a refrigerator.

Green Tomato Chutney

Ingredients

12 small unripe green tomatoes, chopped
1 medium apple
1 inch cinnamon
1 black cardamom
2-3 green cardamoms
2-3 black peppercorns
1 medium onion, peeled and chopped
3-4 garlic cloves
Salt to taste
¾ cup cider or white vinegar
½ cup sugar

Method

1. Peel, core and chop the apples. Tie the cinnamon, black and green cardamoms and peppercorns in a piece of muslin to make a *potli*.
2. Place the tomatoes, apples, *masala potli*, onion and garlic in a heavy-bottomed saucepan. Add salt, half the vinegar and one cup of water, and bring the mixture to a boil. Lower the heat and simmer for twenty minutes, stirring frequently. Remove the *masala potli*.
3. Dissolve the sugar in the remaining vinegar and add to the pan. Simmer, stirring, for twenty minutes. Transfer the hot chutney into a sterilized jar and seal while hot.

Mixed Fruit Chutney

Ingredients

1 large apple, chopped
4 plums, stoned and chopped
1 mango, peeled, stoned and chopped
1 cup dates, stoned and chopped
4 pineapple slices, cut into ½-inch pieces
¼ cup raisins
2 inches ginger, peeled and chopped
½ teaspoon cumin seeds
½ teaspoon coriander seeds
½ teaspoon onion seeds
½ teaspoon aniseed
1 inch cinnamon stick
15-16 almonds, sliced
¼ cup cider vinegar
1 cup brown sugar/jaggery
1 teaspoon red chilli powder
Salt to taste

Method

1. Combine the cumin seeds, coriander seeds, onion seeds, aniseed and cinnamon in a deep, large microwave-safe bowl and roast, uncovered, on Microwave HIGH (100%) for five minutes. Roast the almonds to light brown on Microwave HIGH (100%).

2. Add the apple, plums, mango, dates, pineapple, raisins, ginger and vinegar. Cover and cook on Microwave HIGH (100%) for two minutes.
3. Add the brown sugar/jaggery, chilli powder and salt and cover the bowl. Cook, covered, for a further twenty minutes on Microwave HIGH (100%), stirring occasionally.
4. Allow to cool and pour into a sterlized container. Keep in a refrigerator.

Chef's Tip

If the chutney becomes too thick during cooking, add the reserved pineapple juice. But if at the end of twenty minutes the chutney is not thick enough, uncover the bowl and continue to cook for another two to three minutes.

Til Ki Chutney

Ingredients

100 grams sesame seeds

4 green chillies

1½ tablespoons Tamarind Pulp (page 42)

Salt to taste

3 tablespoons chopped fresh coriander

Seasoning

1 teaspoon oil

½ teaspoon skinless split black gram

3 dried red chillies, broken into bits

¼ teaspoon cumin seeds

¼ teaspoon mustard seeds

6 curry leaves

Method

1. Lightly roast the sesame seeds in a *kadai* and set aside to cool.
2. Grind the sesame seeds and green chillies to a coarse paste.
3. Add the tamarind pulp, salt and fresh coriander and mix well. Transfer the chutney to a bowl.
4. Heat the oil in a *kadai*, add the black gram, red chillies, cumin seeds, mustard seeds and curry leaves. When the mustard seeds begin to splutter, pour the sizzling spices over the ground paste, mix and serve.

Burnt Garlic And Mint Chutney

Ingredients

20-25 garlic cloves

3 cups fresh mint, hand torn

1 tablespoon oil

½ teaspoon black salt

1 inch ginger, roughly chopped

2 green chillies, roughly chopped

1½ cups yogurt, whisked

1 tablespoon lemon juice

Salt to taste

Method

1. Heat the oil in a pan, add the garlic and sauté. Sprinkle the black salt and sauté till well-browned.
2. Place the fresh mint in a processor. Add the ginger, green chillies, sautéed garlic and two tablespoons of water and grind to a fine paste.
3. Add the paste to the yogurt and mix well. Add the lemon juice and salt and mix.
4. Pass the mixture through a piece of muslin, squeezing well to get a smooth chutney.
5. Serve chilled.

Ginger And Tomato Chutney

Ingredients

1 inch ginger, chopped

2 large ripe red tomatoes, chopped

1 teaspoon oil

1 small onion, chopped

½ tablespoon sesame seeds, roasted and powdered

½ tablespoon peanuts, roasted and powdered

½ teaspoon cumin seeds, powdered

1 teaspoon red chilli powder

½ tablespoon grated jaggery

Salt to taste

Method

1. Heat the oil in a pan. Add the tomatoes, ginger and onion. Cook on medium heat till the mixture becomes brown and homogeneous. This may take around twenty minutes. Let it cool.
2. Add the sesame seed, peanut, cumin seed and chilli powders, jaggery and salt and grind to a paste.
3. Store in an airtight bottle and use as required.

Ginger And Tomato Thuvayal

Ingredients

1½ inches ginger, roughly chopped

6 medium tomatoes, roughly chopped

6 tablespoons oil

1 teaspoon mustard seeds

¼ teaspoon asafoetida

10 dried red chillies, broken into large bits

3 teaspoons skinless split black gram

Salt to taste

Method

1. Heat the oil in a pan and add the mustard seeds and asafoetida. As the mustard seeds begin to splutter, add the red chillies and split black gram and sauté till lightly browned.
2. Add the tomatoes, ginger and salt. Stir and cook on low heat till the tomatoes begin to soften. Set aside to cool. Grind the mixture to a slightly coarse texture and serve.

Chef's Tip

Adjust the chillies to suit your personal taste. You can add some garlic to this mixture for a different taste.

Red Chilli-Garlic Chutney

Ingredients

10 dried red chillies, seeded

12 large garlic cloves, peeled and chopped

2 teaspoons lemon juice

Sea salt to taste

1 teaspoon cumin powder

Method

1. Soak the red chillies in one-and-a-half cups of water for half an hour. Drain.
2. Grind the red chillies and garlic cloves with lemon juice to a fine paste. Add a little water if necessary.
3. Add sea salt and cumin powder and mix well.

Spicy Garlic Chutney

Ingredients

8 garlic cloves

¾ cup coconut, grated

5 whole Bedgi red chilies, roasted

Salt to taste

½ teaspoon cumin seeds

2 tablespoons Tamarind Pulp (page 42)

Method

1. Grind the garlic, coconut and roasted red chilies with very little water.
2. Add the salt, cumin seeds and tamarind pulp and process in a blender to a fine paste.
3. Cover and store refrigerated. Best consumed in a day or two.

Plum Chutney

Ingredients

8-10 medium ripe plums, seeded and puréed

Salt to taste

½ cup jaggery, grated

½ teaspoon rock salt

1 teaspoon red chilli powder

1 teaspoon roasted cumin powder

6-8 dates, stoned and chopped

Method

1. Pour the plum purée into a thick-bottomed pan and bring to a boil. Add the salt, jaggery, rock salt and chilli powder and stir well.
2. Lower the heat and simmer on medium heat for ten minutes or till the mixture thickens. Stir in the cumin powder and simmer for two to three minutes.
3. Add the dates and mix well. Add one-fourth cup of water and cook for two more minutes, stirring continuously. Remove from heat, cool thoroughly and store in a sterilized, airtight glass jar.

Keerai Chutney

Ingredients

1 medium bunch (250 grams) of spinach, roughly chopped

1 teaspoon oil

1 tablespoon skinless split black gram

1 tablespoon split Bengal gram

4 dried red chillies

¼ teaspoon asafoetida

1 medium onion, chopped

1 medium tomato, chopped

1 green chilli, chopped

4 tablespoons grated coconut

1 teaspoon Tamarind Pulp (page 42)

Salt to taste

Method

1. Heat the oil in a pan. Add the split black gram and split Bengal gram and roast till golden brown. Add the red chillies, asafoetida, onion, tomato and green chilli.
2. Sauté for five minutes. Add the spinach, coconut, tamarind pulp and salt. Mix well. Remove from heat and cool. Grind to a fine paste and serve.

Note: The Tamil word for spinach and other greens is *keerai*.

Gongura Chutney

Ingredients

1 bunch (250 grams) roselle leaves

3 tablespoons oil

10 garlic cloves, chopped

1½ teaspoons red chilli powder

½ teaspoon mustard seeds

½ teaspoon sesame seeds

½ teaspoon roasted cumin powder

½ teaspoon coriander powder

1 tablespoon Tamarind Pulp (page 42)

Salt to taste

Method

1. Heat two tablespoons of oil in a pan and sauté the garlic till lightly browned. Add the roselle leaves and continue to sauté for ten minutes.
2. Heat the remaining oil in a separate pan and sauté the chilli powder, mustard seeds, sesame seeds, roasted cumin powder and coriander powder for half a minute. Add the tamarind pulp and sautéed roselle leaves.
3. Add half a cup of water and salt and cook till it attains the consistency of chutney. Cool and store in an airtight jar.

Note: Gongura is the Telugu word for roselle leaves.

Peanut Chutney

Ingredients

1 cup roasted peanuts, skinless
4 medium onions, roughly chopped
8-10 garlic cloves, roughly chopped
3 tablespoons oil
4-5 whole red chillies
½ lemon-sized ball tamarind
¼ teaspoon asafoetida
Salt to taste

Method

1. Heat the oil in a pan, add the chopped onions and garlic and sauté for four to five minutes or until they turn golden brown in colour.
2. Add the roasted peanuts, red chillies, tamarind, asafoetida and salt to taste. Stir well and cook for one minute. Remove from heat and cool to room temperature.
3. Grind the mixture to slightly coarse chutney, adding a little water.
4. Store in a refrigerator.

Green Chutney

Ingredients

1 cup fresh coriander, chopped

½ cup fresh mint, chopped

2-3 green chillies, chopped

Black salt to taste

¼ teaspoon sugar

1 teaspoon lemon juice

Method

1. In a blender, process the chopped coriander and mint with the chopped green chillies. Make a smooth paste using a little water if required.
2. Add the black salt and sugar. Transfer to a bowl and stir in the lemon juice.

Variation: Add one cup of yogurt to two tablespoons of chutney for a completely different flavour.

Chef's Tip

You can use crushed dried pomegranate seeds or dried mango powder instead of lemon juice. In season unripe green mango is a good substitute.

Date And Tamarind Chutney

Ingredients

15-20 dates, stoned and roughly chopped

1 cup Tamarind Pulp (page 42)

2 teaspoons cumin seeds

¼ teaspoon fennel seeds

½ cup grated jaggery

2 teaspoons red chilli powder

1 teaspoon dried ginger powder

1 teaspoon black salt

Salt to taste

Method

1. Dry-roast the cumin seeds and fennel seeds. Cool slightly and grind together to a powder.
2. Mix together the dates, jaggery, tamarind pulp, cumin and fennel powder, chilli powder, dried ginger powder, black salt, salt to taste and four cups of water.
3. Cook on medium heat till it comes to a boil. Lower the heat and continue to cook for six to eight minutes. Cool and serve.

Tetuler Chaatni

Ingredients

500 grams tamarind

½ cup mustard oil

1 teaspoon roasted *panch phoron* powder

400 grams jaggery, grated

Salt to taste

½ teaspoon black pepper powder

1 teaspoon roasted red chilli powder

1 tablespoon raisins

Method

1. Soak the tamarind in half cup warm water, remove the pulp, strain and reserve.
2. Heat the mustard oil in a pan and add the *panch phoron* powder and tamarind pulp and cook for few minutes. Add the jaggery and cook till it melts; season it with the salt, black pepper powder and roasted chilli powder. Cook for two more minutes.
3. Serve the *chaatni* garnished with the raisins.

Note: 1. *Panch phoron* is a mixture of equal quantities of mustard seeds, cumin seeds, fenugreek seeds, fennel seeds and caraway seeds.

2. Tetul is the Bengali word for tamarind.

Sarson Ki Chutney

Ingredients

½ cup mustard seeds

1½ cups + 4 tablespoons vinegar

Salt to taste

1 tablespoon sugar

¼ teaspoon turmeric powder

Method

1. Grind the mustard seeds with four tablespoons of vinegar to a fine paste.
2. Pour one-and a-half cups vinegar in a pan. Add the salt, sugar and turmeric powder and bring to a boil. Add the mustard paste and cook for fifteen to twenty minutes or till thick.
3. Cool and serve.

Chef's Tip

For best results mature for two days and serve.

Black Bean Sauce

Ingredients

3 tablespoons black beans, boiled

½ inch fresh ginger, peeled and roughly chopped

1 garlic clove, peeled and roughly chopped

2 tablespoons vinegar

1 tablespoon soy sauce

Salt to taste

Pepper powder to taste

1 teaspoon sugar

¾ cup Vegetable Stock (see below)

2 teaspoons cornflour

1 teaspoon butter

Method

1. Mix the cooked black beans, ginger, garlic, vinegar, soy sauce, salt, pepper powder, sugar and half the vegetable stock; purée the mixture in a blender.
2. Transfer the mixture to a pan; bring to a boil, reduce the heat and simmer for a while. Mix the cornflour with the remaining vegetable stock and add to the purée. Cook, stirring continuously, till thick. Melt the butter and stir into the thickened sauce.

Vegetable Stock

Peel, wash and chop 1 onion, ½ medium carrot, 2-3 inch stalk celery and 2-3 garlic cloves. Place in a pan with 1 bay leaf, 5-6 peppercorns, 2-3 cloves and five cups of water and bring to a boil. Lower heat and simmer for fifteen minutes and strain. Cool and store in a refrigerator till further use.

Quick Tomato Sauce

Ingredients

6 medium tomatoes, quartered
1 small carrot, cut into ¼-inch cubes
1 small onion, chopped
6-8 garlic cloves, crushed
2 tablespoons oil
10 fresh basil leaves
1 teaspoon black pepper powder
Salt to taste
½ teaspoon sugar

Method

1. Heat the oil in a microwave-safe bowl, uncovered, for one minute on Microwave HIGH (100%). Remove from the oven and add the carrot, onion and garlic to the oil. Cover and cook on Microwave HIGH (100%) for six minutes.
2. Add the tomatoes with their juice, fresh basil leaves, pepper powder, salt and sugar. Cover and cook on Microwave HIGH (100%) for six minutes, stirring halfway through the cooking time.
3. Remove and let it cool. Purée the mixture in a blender. Store in a glass bottle.

Sweet Chilli Sauce

Ingredients

18-20 Kashmiri red chillies, seeded

2 medium tomatoes, chopped

3-4 garlic cloves, chopped

2 tablespoons sugar

1 tablespoon oil

1 tablespoon soy sauce

Salt to taste

Method

1. Grind together the red chillies, tomatoes and garlic into a smooth paste.
2. Combine the sugar and oil in a microwave-safe bowl and cook, uncovered, on Microwave HIGH (100%) for two minutes. Remove.
3. Add the paste, soy sauce, salt to taste and one cup of water. Mix well. Cook, uncovered, on Microwave MEDIUM (70%) for two minutes.
4. Remove and stir once. Cook, uncovered, for two minutes more. Remove and serve when cooled.

Sweet And Sour Sauce

Ingredients

1 cup tomato ketchup

⅓ cup malt vinegar

2 teaspoons soy sauce

¼ cup sugar

Black pepper powder to taste

Salt to taste

2 tablespoons cornflour

Method

1. Mix all the ingredients with two cups of water in a pan and stir to mix well.
2. Gradually bring the mixture to a boil, stirring continuously.
3. Lower the heat and simmer for two to three minutes.
4. Cool and store.

Chef's Tip

Use plain vinegar if malt vinegar is not available.

White Sauce

Ingredients

1½ tablespoons refined flour
2 tablespoons butter
1 medium onion
1 bay leaf
2 cloves
1½ cups milk
Salt to taste
¼ teaspoon white pepper powder
A small pinch of grated nutmeg

Method

1. Melt one-and-a-half tablespoons of butter in a thick-bottomed pan.
2. Add the flour; stir and cook the roux (butter-flour mixture) over low heat with a wooden spoon. When it develops a sandy texture, remove from heat and cool. Peel the onion. Wrap a bay leaf around it studding it with cloves at the two ends.
3. Bring the milk to a boil with the onion. Simmer for a couple of minutes and discard the onion. Pour the boiling hot milk into the cold roux, stirring continuously, to prevent lumps from forming.
4. Simmer gently for two minutes. Add the seasoning and nutmeg. Melt the remaining butter and gently pour over the top of the sauce to prevent a skin from forming.

Sichuan Sauce

Ingredients

10-12 dried red chillies, stems removed

½ cup oil

10 garlic cloves, finely chopped

2 green chillies, finely chopped

2 spring onions, finely chopped

1 inch ginger, grated

2-3 inches celery stalk, finely chopped

3 tablespoons tomato ketchup

Salt to taste

2 teaspoons white vinegar

Method

1. Boil the red chillies in one cup of water for five to seven minutes. Drain the chillies, cool and grind to a fine paste.
2. Heat the oil in a pan; add the garlic, green chillies, spring onions and ginger and sauté for one minute. Add the red chilli paste and continue to sauté for a few more seconds. Add the celery, tomato ketchup and salt and stir well to mix.
3. Stir in the vinegar and simmer for one minute. When the oil rises to the surface, take the pan off the heat. Cool, bottle and store.
4. Sichuan sauce will keep for a month if there is oil covering the surface.

Pepper Chili Sauce

Ingredients

3 medium green capsicums, cut into ¼-inch cubes

7-8 black peppercorns, freshly crushed

1 teaspoon red chilli powder

6 medium tomatoes, chopped

1 medium onion, chopped

4-5 cloves

1 inch cinnamon

½ cup brown sugar

¼ cup cider vinegar

1 bay leaf

Salt to taste

Method

1. Place the cloves and cinnamon in a microwave-safe plate and dry-roast on Microwave HIGH (100%) for two minutes. Grind to a coarse powder.
2. Place the tomatoes, onion, brown sugar, cider vinegar (replace with any other vinegar if not available), clove-cinnamon powder, chilli powder and bay leaf in a large microwave-safe bowl. Cover and cook on Microwave HIGH (100%) for fifteen minutes. Remove.
3. Stir in the capsicums, salt and freshly crushed peppercorns. Cook, uncovered, on Microwave HIGH (100%) for fifteen minutes or until the mixture thickens. Discard the bay leaf and pour into a hot, sterilized jar. Seal and cover. Best stored in refrigerator.

Sweet Coriander Sauce

Ingredients

3½ tablespoons fresh coriander, finely chopped

1 tablespoon cornflour

1 teaspoon oil

3 garlic cloves, finely chopped

Salt to taste

½ teaspoon black pepper powder

⅓ cup sugar

2 teaspoons lemon juice

Method

1. Mix the cornflour with half a cup of water and set aside.
2. Heat the oil in a pan; add the chopped garlic and sauté for one minute.
3. Add one cup of water, chopped fresh coriander, salt, pepper powder, sugar and lemon juice and stir to mix well.
4. Bring the mixture to a boil, lower the heat and add the cornflour mixture.
5. Stir and simmer till the sauce thickens. Cool and store.

Cheese And Herb Dip

Ingredients

1 cup cheese, grated

¼ cup milk

Salt to taste

¼ teaspoon white pepper powder

¼ teaspoon dried oregano

¼ teaspoon dried thyme

Method

1. Mix the cheese and milk.
2. Heat the mixture in double boiler so that the cheese melts and the mixture gets a smooth consistency.
3. Season with salt, white pepper powder and dried herbs. Use it immediately or else it will thicken again.

Note: A double boiler is a pan with a wide mouth filled with boiling water into which smaller pan is placed.

Beans 'n' Chilli Dip

Ingredients

1 cup red kidney beans, boiled
2 green chillies, chopped
1 medium onion, chopped
1 medium tomato, chopped
4 garlic cloves, chopped
1 tablespoon lemon juice
Salt to taste
½ teaspoon red chilli powder
2 tablespoons tomato ketchup
1 teaspoon Tabasco sauce
2 tablespoons olive oil
3-4 black peppercorns, crushed
2 tablespoons fresh coriander, chopped

Method

1. Process the kidney beans in a blender to a coarse paste. Transfer to a bowl.
2. Add the green chillies, onion, tomato, garlic, lemon juice, salt, chilli powder, tomato ketchup, Tabasco sauce, olive oil and crushed peppercorns; mix thoroughly.
3. Garnish with fresh coriander and serve with nachos, wafers or crudités (cut raw vegetables).

Avocado Dip

Ingredients

1 medium avocado

1 small onion, chopped

¼ cup fresh coriander, chopped

1 medium green capsicum, chopped

Salt to taste

4 medium tomatoes, chopped

Method

1. Cut the avocado in half and remove the stone.
2. Process half the onion, half the fresh coriander, the capsicum and salt in a blender to a smooth paste.
3. Scoop out the flesh of the avocado and mash roughly with the paste.
4. Add the tomatoes, remaining onion and fresh coriander. Mix well and serve immediately with nachos, crackers or crudités (cut raw vegetables).

Salsa Fresca

Ingredients

4 medium tomatoes

1 medium onion, finely chopped

2 jalapeño chillies, finely chopped

Juice of half lemon

2 teaspoons olive oil

1 teaspoon vinegar

½ teaspoon salt

½ teaspoon dried oregano, crushed

¼ cup fresh coriander, roughly chopped

Method

1. Wash and remove eyes of the tomatoes, make a cross slit on the bottom side and immerse in boiling water for half a minute. Drain the tomatoes, peel, deseed and chop them roughly.
2. In a medium-sized bowl, combine the tomatoes, onion and chillies.
3. Add the lemon juice, olive oil, vinegar, salt and oregano.
4. Mix well and let the sauce stand for at least two hours to blend the flavours.
5. Stir in the chopped coriander. Serve at room temperature with your choice of snacks or as a dip for your cocktail snacks.

Melting Cheese Dip

Ingredients

1½ cups processed cheese, grated

½ cup milk

1 tablespoon tinned jalapeños, drained and chopped

Salt to taste

½ teaspoon Tabasco sauce

1 tablespoon fresh coriander, chopped

Method

1. Heat the milk in a double boiler. Gradually add the cheese and cook stirring continuously, to get a mixture of smooth texture.
2. Add the jalapeños, salt and Tabasco sauce. Mix well.
3. Remove from the heat, add the fresh coriander and stir to blend well. Serve immediately.

Peanut Yogurt Dip

Ingredients

¼ cup peanuts, roasted and crushed coarsely

2 cups yogurt

Salt to taste

2 whole red chillies, crushed

2 tablespoons fresh coriander, chopped finely

¼ cup cream

Method

1. Hang the yogurt overnight in a piece of muslin to remove excess moisture. This process can be carried out in the refrigerator to avoid the yogurt from getting too sour.
2. Place the drained yogurt in a mixing bowl; whisk it to get a smooth texture.
3. Season with salt and add the crushed red chillies, peanuts and chopped coriander. Whisk in the cream and mix well.

Thousand Island Dip

Ingredients

1 cup Mayonnaise (see below)

1 pickled gherkin, chopped

2 small shallots, chopped

2 tablespoons tomato ketchup

1 teaspoon Tabasco sauce

1 tablespoon lemon juice

Salt to taste

3-4 black peppercorns, crushed

2 tablespoons fresh parsley, chopped

Method

1. Add the gherkin, shallots and tomato ketchup to the mayonnaise and mix well. Add Tabasco sauce, lemon juice, salt and crushed black peppercorns. Mix well with wooden spoon.
2. Check the seasoning and add the parsley. Transfer the dip into a bowl, cover and allow to chill in a refrigerator. Serve/use chilled.

Mayonnaise

Place 1 egg yolk, salt to taste, ¼ teaspoon each white pepper powder, mustard powder and sugar and 1 teaspoon vinegar in a clean bowl and mix thoroughly with a whisk. Alternatively, process the mixture in a blender. Add 1 cup of oil, a little at a time, whisking or blending continuously, until all the oil is incorporated. Add 1 teaspoon lemon juice and adjust seasoning. Store in an airtight jar in a refrigerator.

Roasted Pepper And Tomato Dip

Ingredients

1 medium red capsicum, seeded and quartered

5 medium tomatoes, seeded and quartered

5-6 garlic cloves

Salt to taste

2 teaspoons sugar

2 tablespoons lemon juice

Fresh parsley sprig, for garnishing

Method

1. Preheat an oven to 180ºC/350ºF/Gas Mark 4. Arrange the red capsicum and tomato quarters along with the garlic in a baking tray. Sprinkle salt over them.
2. Bake in the preheated oven for twenty to twenty-five minutes. Remove from the oven and cool. Peel the capsicum, tomatoes and garlic. Chop them finely.
3. Heat a non-stick pan and roast the garlic for a minute. Add the capsicum and tomatoes and cook for two minutes. Add the salt and sugar. Mix well.
4. Cook for another two minutes and add the lemon juice. Mix again. Serve, garnished with a sprig of parsley.

GLOSSARY

English	Hindi
Almonds	badam
Aniseed	saunf
Apple	saeb
Asafoetida	hing
Bay leaves	tej patta
Bengal gram, split	chana dal
Black gram, skinless split	dhuli urad dal
Black gram, split	urad dal
Brinjal	baingan
Carom seeds	ajwain
Carrot	gajar
Cauliflower	phoolgobhi
Celery	ajmud
Chickpea	Kabuli chana
Chillies, dried red	sookhi lal mirch
Chillies, green	hari mirch
Cinnamon	dalchini
Cloves	laung

English	Hindi
Coconut	nariyal
Coriander seeds	dhania
Cream	malai
Cumin seeds	jeera
Curry leaves	kadhi patta
Dates	khajoor
Fennel seeds	saunf
Fenugreek seeds	methi
Fenugreek seeds, split	methi dal
Fig	anjeer
Fresh basil leaves	tulsi ke patte
Fresh coriander leaves	hara dhania
Fresh mint leaves	pudina
Fresh spinach leaves	palak
Garlic cloves	lehsun ki kaliyan
Ginger, dried	sonth
Ginger, fresh	adrak
Honey	shahad

GLOSSARY

English	Hindi
Indian gooseberries	amla
Jaggery	gur
Lemon	nimbu
Mango powder, dried	amchur
Mustard seeds	rai
Mustard seeds, skinless split	bina chilke ka sarson ka dal
Nutmeg	jaiphal
Olive	jaitun
Onion seeds	kalonji
Onions	pyaaz
Orange	narangi/santara
Parsley	ajmoda
Peanuts	moongphali
Peppercorns, black	kali mirch
Peppercorns, white	safed mirch
Pineapple	ananas
Plums	aloo bukhare
Pomegranate seeds, dried	anardana
Raisins	kishmish
Red chilli, dried	sookhi lal mirch
Red kidney beans	rajma
Refined flour	maida
Roselle leaves	khatta bhaji
Salt, black	kala namak
Salt, rock	sendha namak
Salt, sea	samudri namak
Sesame seeds, white	safed til
Shallots	sambhar onions
Sugar	cheeni
Tamarind	imli
Tamarind pulp	imli ka gooda
Tomato	tamatar
Tomato purée	pisa hua tamatar
Tomato, unripe green	kachche tamatar
Turmeric	haldi
Turnip	shalgam
Vinegar	sirka
Yogurt	dahi